Editor
Barbara M. Wally, M.S.

Editorial Project Manager
Ina Massler Levin, M.A.

Editor in Chief
Sharon Coan, M.S. Ed.

Cover Artist
Sue Fullam

Art Coordinator
Denice Adorno

Creative Director
Elayne Roberts

Imaging
Ralph Olmedo, Jr.

Product Manager
Phil Garcia

Publishers
Rachelle Cracchiolo, M.S. Ed.
Mary Dupuy Smith, M.S. Ed.

How to Make a Book

Grades 6–8

Author

Shirley E. Myers

Teacher Created Materials, Inc.
6421 Industry Way
Westminster, CA 92683
www.teachercreated.com

ISBN-1-57690-487-3

©2000 Teacher Created Materials, Inc.
Reprinted, 2000
Made in U.S.A.

Table of Contents

Introduction

How to Make a Book Report is a step-by-step guide for students as they write and present a variety of book reports. This book contains a framework in which students can learn an organized, responsible and accountable way to do book report writing. The student work pages encourage an organized and pro-active approach to reading and to writing book reports. *How to Make a Book Report* is a tool to encourage, stimulate, develop, and nurture the enjoyment of reading.

The units presented in this book may be used in any order and are readily adaptable to cross-curricular planning. The individual units may be combined to create a comprehensive reading/writing plan for the school year. Individual reports and presentations can also be used to create a student portfolio.

Getting Started—Breaking Out of the Routine

In some ways reading is similar to cooking. Some people like to cook a good stew, letting the pot simmer for hours as aromas build and flavors blend. Then they take the time to savor their meal just as some readers take the time to savor their reading. Other people like a fast-food meal that is ready in moments and consumed in very little time, just as some readers like to do their reading, quickly and with the least amount of effort necessary. A person with no appetite probably does not cook and may have an empty pot sitting on a cold stove.

Food for Thought: If your students are expected to "cook up" some good book reports, it is important to help them develop an appetite for reading. Only then will they have the right "ingredients" that will enable them to write good book reports.

The Recipe for Good Book Reports

- one healthy interest in reading

- a number of well-chosen books to read

- a pro-active reading style

- a step-by-step approach to book report writing

Directions: Mix the ingredients thoroughly; allow to simmer throughout the school year.

Think of yourself as the "teacher/cook" whose "recipe" will help create life-long readers of good books and skilled writers of good reports!

Student Reading Survey

	Yes	No
1. Do you enjoy reading?		
2. Is reading easy for you?		
3. Do you have a library card?		
4. Do you use the public library?		
5. Do you use your school library?		
6. Do you think books are important?		
7. Do you know how to use the Dewey Decimal System?		
8. Have you read a book from cover to cover in the last three months?		
9. Is there a time of day that you enjoy reading?		
10. Would you be interested in learning about careers in the field of writing?		
11. Have you ever met an author?		
12. Have you ever seen a movie that was based on a book?		
13. Do you remember what you have read?		
14. Have you ever discussed a book with another person?		
15. Have you ever read a book to someone younger?		
16. Do you remember a time when you enjoyed having someone read to you?		
17. Do you always have a book to read?		
18. Do you have a favorite author?		
19. Do you think you have become a better reader in the past year?		

20. Do you read a daily newspaper or a weekly/monthly magazine? _____

21. Approximately how old were you when you began to read? _____

22. What do you like about reading? _____

23. Is there anything you dislike about reading? _____

24. Circle the kinds of reading you like to do. You may add to this list.

adventure	humor	mystery	humor	myths/legends
poetry	animals	autobiography	folk tales/fables	romance
science fiction	biography	travel	fantasy	sports

Titles _____

_____

Reading Record

To Do: When you begin reading a new book, complete the form below. Use this information as you schedule future reading along with homework and other activities.

Book Title: _____ Starting Date:_____

Date of reading session	Time spent reading	Number of pages read
1.		
2.		
3.		
4.		
5.		
6.		
7.		
8.		
9.		
10.		
11.		
12.		
13.		
14.		
15.		
16.		
17.		
18.		
19.		
20.		
21.		
22.		
23.		
24.		
25.		

Date I completed reading my book: _____ Total number of reading sessions: _____

Total number of reading hours: _____

Did I allow enough time to read or was I rushed?_____

What changes will I make in reading my next book? _____

What was the major problem I experienced in this reading?_____

Food for Thought: By keeping a record of your reading times, you can get a realistic idea of the amount of time it will take you to read books in the future.

Suggested Reading

How do you choose a book to read? Do you browse through the bookstore or library shelves looking at the covers? Do you look in the library's card catalog for a particular subject, title, or author? Perhaps you take the advice of friends, or read the on-line book reviews. The list below is organized by categories, and contains a wide variety of titles. Use it as a guide when you select a book to read for a book report.

Titles preceded by an asterisk (*) are Newbery Award winners.

Biographies/Autobiographies

Brian's Song. William Blinn. Turtleback, 1989.

Christopher Reeve. Libby Hughes. Dillion Press, 1997.

Death Be Not Proud: A Memoir. John Gunther. HarperPerennial Library, 1998.

Diary of a Young Girl. Anne Frank. Bantam, 1993.

Farewell to Manzanar. Jeanne W. Houston. Turtleback, 1983.

The Hiding Place. Corrie Ten Boom. Fleming H. Revell Co., 1996.

The Miracle Worker. William Gibson. Bantam, 1984.

Ryan White: My Own Story. Ryan White. Signet, 1992.

Zlata's Diary: A Child's Life in Sarajevo. Zlata Filipovic. Penguin, 1997.

Animal Stories

Big Red. Jim Kjelgaard. Bantam Skylark, 1992.

Black Beauty. Anna Sewell. Random House, 1986.

The Black Stallion. Walter Farley. Random House, 1991.

Born Free. Joy Adamson. Random House, 1987.

Call of the Wild. Jack London. Tor Books, 1990.

The Incredible Journey. Sheila Burnford. Yearling Books, 1996.

It's Like This, Cat. Emily Neville. HarperTrophy, 1964.

Lassie Come Home. Eric Knight. Henry Holt & Co., 1995.

My Friend Flicka. Mary O'Hara. Turtleback, 1988.

National Velvet. Enid Bagnold. Flare, 1991.

Old Yeller. Fred Gipson. HarperTrophy, 1990.

The Red Pony. John Steinbeck. Penguin, 1993.

**Shiloh.* Phyllis Reynolds Naylor. Yearling Books, 1992.

**The Voyages of Doctor Doolittle.* Hugh Lofting. Tor Books, 1998.

Watership Down. Richard Adams. Avon, 1989.

When the Legends Die. Hal Borland. Bantam Starfire, 1984.

Where the Red Fern Grows. Wilson Rawls. Bantam, 1984.

The Yearling. Marjorie Kinnan Rawlings. Aladdin Paperbacks, 1988.

Mysteries

The Dragon in the Ghetto Caper. E. L. Konigsburg. Aladdin, 1998.

**From the Mixed Up Files of Mrs. Basil E. Frankweiler.* E.L. Konigsburg. Yearling Books, 1967.

House of Dies Drear. Virginia Hamilton. Aladdin, 1984.

Up From Jericho Tel. E. L. Konigsburg. Aladdin, 1998.

**The Westing Game.* Ellen Raskin. Dutton, 1979.

Mystery Series

The Baby-Sitters Club Mysteries. Ann Martin. Apple.

The Boxcar Children. Gertrude Chandler Warner. Albert Whitman.

Nancy Drew and the Hardy Boys Super Mysteries. Carolyn Keene. Archway.

Jenny McGrady Mysteries. Patricia H. Rushford. Bethany House.

Fiction

Best Christmas Pageant Ever. Barbara Robinson. HarperTrophy, 1988.

Charlie and the Chocolate Factory. Roald Dahl. Puffin, 1998.

**The Giver.* Lois Lowry. Houghton, 1994.

Harriet the Spy. Louise Fitzhugh. HarperTrophy, 1996.

Hatchet. Gary Paulsen. Aladdin, 1996.

I Heard the Owl Call My Name. Margaret Craven. Turtleback, 1993.

In the Year of the Boar and Jackie Robinson. Betty Bao Lord. HarperTrophy, 1986.

Little House on the Prairie. Laura Ingalls Wilder. HarperCollins, 1953.

My Side of the Mountain. Jean Craighead George. Viking, 1991.

The Outsiders. S. E. Hinton. Puffin, 1997.

**Roll of Thunder, Hear My Cry.* Mildred Taylor. Dial, 1977.

Suggested Reading *(cont.)*

Fiction *(cont.)*

Sarah, Plain and Tall. Patricia MacLachlan. Harper, 1986.

Secret Garden. Frances Hodgson Burnett. Harper Trophy, 1987.

Sounder. William H. Armstrong. Harper, 1970.

Summer of the Swans. Betsy Byars. Viking, 1971.

Tuck Everlasting. Natalie Babbitt. Farrar, Straus & Giroux, 1986.

Historical Fiction

Across Five Aprils. Irene Hunt. Berkley Publishing Group, 1991.

The Bronze Bow. Elizabeth George Speare. Houghton, 1962.

Catherine, Called Birdy. Karen Cushman. Clarion, 1995.

Cowboys (Reflections of a Black Cowboy). Robert Miller. Silver Burdett, 1998.

Dragonwings. Laurence Yep. HarperTrophy, 1989.

Island of the Blue Dolphins. Scott O'Dell. Houghton, 1961.

Johnny Tremain. Esther Forbes. Houghton, 1944.

Julie of the Wolves. Jean Craighead George. Harper & Row, 1973.

The Light in the Forest. Conrad Richter. Juniper, 1995.

M.C. Higgins the Great. Virginia Hamilton. Aladdin, 1998.

Onion John. Joseph Krumgold. Crowell, 1960.

Sarah Bishop. Scott O'Dell. Point, 1991.

The Serpent Never Sleeps. Scott O'Dell. Juniper, 1990.

Shane. Jack Warner Shaefer. Bantam Starfire, 1983.

Sign of the Beaver. Elizabeth George Speare. Yearling, 1994.

The Slave Dancer. Paula Fox. Bradbury, 1974.

Up a Road Slowly. Irene Hunt. Follett, 1967.

A Way Through the Sea (Young Underground Collection, Book 1). Robert Elmer. Bethany House, 1994.

Where the Lilies Bloom. Vera and Bill Cleaver. HarperTrophy, 1989.

Science Fiction/Fantasy

Animal Farm. George Orwell. Turtleback, 1996.

Bridge to Terabithia. Katherine Paterson. Crowell, 1978.

The Grey King. Susan Cooper. McElderry/Atheneum, 1976.

The High King. Lloyd Alexander. Holt, 1969.

Lord of the Rings. J.R.R. Tolkien. Houghton Mifflin, 1991.

The Magician's Nephew (Chronicles of Narnia, Book 6). C.S. Lewis. HarperCollins Juvenile, 1994.

Mrs. Frisby and the Rats of NIMH. Robert C. O'Brien. Atheneum, 1972.

The Time Machine. H.G. Wells. Tor Books, 1995.

A Wrinkle in Time. Madeline L'Engle. Farrar, 1963.

Classics

The Adventures of Huckleberry Finn. Mark Twain. Bantam Classic, 1981.

The Adventures of Robin Hood. Roger Lancelyn Green. Puffin Classics, 1995.

Anne of Green Gables. Lucy Maud Montgomery. Tor Books, 1995.

Around the World in 80 Days. Jules Verne. Turtleback, 1996.

Captains Courageous. Rudyard Kipling. Bantam Classics, 1985.

Great Expectations. Charles Dickens. Tor Books, 1998.

Hound of the Baskervilles. Arthur Conan Doyle. Berkeley Pub Group, 1993.

The Invisible Man. H.G. Wells. Tor Books, 1992.

The Last of the Mohicans. James Fenimore Cooper. Random House, 1993.

The Legend of Sleepy Hollow. Washington Irving. Tor Books, 1990.

Little Women. Louisa May Alcott. Tor Books, 1994.

The Old Man and the Sea. Ernest Hemingway. Scribner, 1995.

The Pearl. John Steinbeck. Penguin, 1993.

The Prince and the Pauper. Mark Twain. Puffin, 1996.

The Red Badge of Courage. Stephen Crane. Tor Books, 1997.

Swiss Family Robinson. Johann David Wyss. Yearling, 1999.

Treasure Island. Robert Louis Stevenson. Bantam Classics, 1992.

Individual Reading Pledge

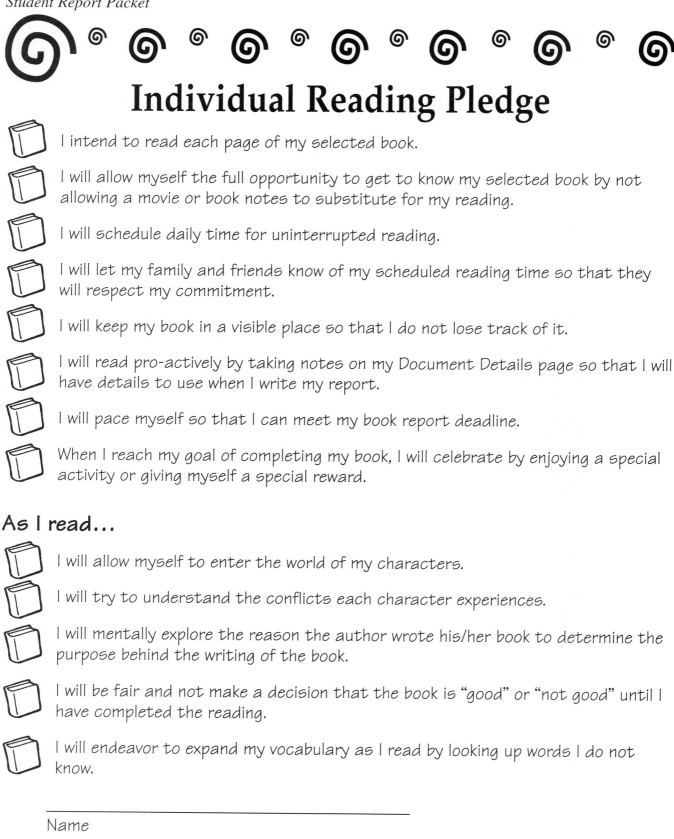

I intend to read each page of my selected book.

I will allow myself the full opportunity to get to know my selected book by not allowing a movie or book notes to substitute for my reading.

I will schedule daily time for uninterrupted reading.

I will let my family and friends know of my scheduled reading time so that they will respect my commitment.

I will keep my book in a visible place so that I do not lose track of it.

I will read pro-actively by taking notes on my Document Details page so that I will have details to use when I write my report.

I will pace myself so that I can meet my book report deadline.

When I reach my goal of completing my book, I will celebrate by enjoying a special activity or giving myself a special reward.

As I read...

I will allow myself to enter the world of my characters.

I will try to understand the conflicts each character experiences.

I will mentally explore the reason the author wrote his/her book to determine the purpose behind the writing of the book.

I will be fair and not make a decision that the book is "good" or "not good" until I have completed the reading.

I will endeavor to expand my vocabulary as I read by looking up words I do not know.

_____

Name

_____

Date

Book Report Log

Date	Title	Author	Genre/Themes	Type of Report

Book Reports and You

There are two facts concerning book reports that every middle-school student needs to know. First, book reports are written in middle school/junior high, high school, and even college. You just can't get away from them. Secondly, good book report writing doesn't just happen. It takes practice!

The pages in this packet are designed to help you learn how to write book reports using the standard format that will be required in high school and college. This step-by-step approach to book report writing will help you grow in the following areas:

Time Management—Once you have tracked how long it takes you to read a book, and how long it takes to prepare a report or project, you can plan ahead. You will not have to read your book and write your report in one night.

Reading Comprehension—You will increase your memory and save time by keeping notes as you read. By recording information and page numbers while you are reading, you will not have to search for needed details once you begin writing your report.

Writing Skills—By following the samples and format, you can express yourself in a way that others, especially your teachers, will understand.

Confidence—Now, you won't view book reports as dreaded assignments.

To Do: As you work through your packet, your teacher will assign a due date for each step. Use this list to keep track of these dates.

Check Points

Process	Due Date
Individual Reading pledge signed	
Pre-writing pages completed	
First draft completed	
Second draft completed	
Final draft turned in	

Chapter-by-Chapter Synopsis

To Do: After you have read a chapter, write one sentence that will help you remember what the chapter was about. Use this page as a review when you begin to write your report.

Chapter	One-sentence synopsis

Documenting Details

To Do: As you read, keep a record of key details and descriptions to use in your book report. Include page numbers for future reference.

People	Page

Places	Page

Events	Page

Conflicts	Page

The Cast of Characters

Every book has a cast of characters, either real or imaginary. They may be major characters, like the protagonist and antagonist, or minor characters, who add color and details to the story. The author reveals the characters to the reader by describing his or her physical attributes, actions and, in some cases, the character's thoughts and motivations.

As each character is introduced, record his or her name and initial description. Add details about each character as they are revealed during the course of the story. Make a note of the pages that refer to each character.

When you have finished the book, review what you have written about the characters. If the character plays a major role in the development of the story, write a capital M on the line before the name. If he or she is a minor character, one who adds interest but is not essential to the story, write a lower case m on the line.

Name	Physical Description	Actions	Page
1.			
2.			
3.			
4.			
5.			
6.			
7.			
8.			
9.			
10.			

Book Talk

To Think About and Do: Literature has its own specialized vocabulary to describe elements of a story. Some of this vocabulary is listed below. As you read, look for examples of each term. Add any other terms you find to the list. By learning these terms and using them often, especially in your reading discussion groups and in your book report writing, you will increase your vocabulary and improve your understanding of the books you read.

Check your knowledge of these terms by using them to complete the puzzle on page 41.

The Reader's List of Literary Terms

allegory	This term means that characters and events in a story represent ideas or principles.
antagonist	This person is an adversary who challenges the main character or hero.
autobiography	This refers to a book that a person writes about his or her own life story.
biography	This is a book that one person writes about another person's life story.
characterization	This term means a description of the qualities and attributes of characters in a story.
climax	This is the word for the story's most intense point.
comedy	This is a book that has humorous themes and/or characters and usually has a happy ending.
conflict	This is a struggle or problem faced by a character. It may be an external conflict, caused by other characters or outside forces, or an internal conflict that comes from problems within the character.
dialogue	This refers to a conversation between characters in a story.
drama	This is a term for a story that is written for performance before an audience; drama can also refer to a situation that has the emotional effect of a play.
dynamic character	This phrase describes a character who changes during the story because of events that occur.
exposition	This is background information about characters and setting that is often given at the beginning of a story.
falling action	This refers to the events which follow the climax or turning point.
fiction	This is literature which uses invented characters and plots to tell a story.
foreshadow	This literary device is used to suggest or indicate a future event.
frame story	This term refers to the technique of placing a story within a story.
genre	This word means a class or category of literature.
metaphor	This is a figure of speech that makes a comparison by using one thing or word to describe another.
memoir	This type of book is an account of the author's personal experiences or an autobiography.

Book Talk *(cont.)*

The Reader's List of Literary Terms *(cont.)*

motif	This is a recurring or dominant theme in literature.
narrative	This form of writing tells a story.
nonfiction	In this form of literature, the story is about real characters and events.
novel	This is the name for a fictional prose narrative that is book-length.
omniscient narrator	In this form, the person telling the story knows everything about the characters and the plot.
personification	In this figure of speech, an inanimate object or abstract idea is given human form.
plot	This term is used for the sequence of events or actions.
point of view	This is the relationship of the person telling the story to the characters and events. If a story is told in the first person point of view, a character within the story relates his or her relationship to the events using the pronoun "I." In a third person point of view story, someone outside the story tells the events, using the pronouns "he" and "she."
protagonist	This is the term used for the main character, or hero, of the story.
pseudonym	This is a fictitious name used by an author as his or her own.
resolution	Also known as the *denouement*, this tells the final outcome of the story.
rising action	This term refers to the events which build toward the climax or turning point.
satire	This refers to using irony, sarcasm, or derision to attack or expose human folly or vice.
sequel	This is the name for a book which follows up on the characters and events of a previous book.
setting	This describes where and when the story takes place.
simile	This figure of speech uses "as" or "like" to make a comparison of two different things.
static character	This term is used for a character who remains the same throughout the story.
subplot	This is a plot within a story that is of lesser importance than the main plot.
symbolism	This refers to an object, person, or place that represents an idea or quality.
synopsis	This is a brief summary of the story told in one's own words.
theme	The main idea of a story, novel, or play; this makes a general statement about life.
tragedy	Literary works of this genre portray calamitous events and have unhappy endings.
turning point	This is a decisive moment in the story, when a significant change occurs.

Writing a Standard Book Report

To Think About: If you were to tell someone about the book you just read, what would you say? What parts of the plot would you share? What would you say about the characters? How would you describe the setting?

A written book report is one way to share information about what you have read with an audience of readers. Use the details you recorded while you were reading to complete your book report.

The Four Parts of a Book Report

Part 1—The Introduction

The introductory paragraph of your report introduces the book to the reader. This paragraph includes the following items:

- book title and author's name
- introduction to the main characters
- description of the setting (time and place)
- introduction to the theme of the story

To Do: Read the samples below to see how information is used in the introduction. Choose one and use it as a pattern to write your own introduction in the practice box.

Remember to underline the title of your book every time you write it. If you are typing, you may italicize the book title instead of underlining it.

Sample 1

Where the Red Fern Grows, written by Wilson Rawls, is the story of 12-year-old Billy and his two dogs, Little Ann and Old Dan. *Where the Red Fern Grows* takes place in a valley in the rugged Ozark Mountains on the banks of the Illinois River in Oklahoma and is a story of love, loyalty, and courage.

Sample 2

Set in a valley in the rugged Ozark Mountains of Oklahoma, *Where the Red Fern Grows* is the story of love and loyalty between a boy and his dogs. The author, Wilson Rawls, writes the story of Little Ann, Old Dan, and Billy (two dogs and a boy), who experience triumph and tragedy in their hunt for raccoons.

Practice Box

_____

_____

_____

_____

Handy Tip of the Day: Use present tense verbs when you write a book report.

Writing a Standard Book Report *(cont.)*

The Four Parts of a Book Report *(cont.)*

Part 2—The Body

The body of a book report retells the story. Use your own words to give information about the following:

Highlights of the plot _____

_____

_____

Each character's involvement in the plot _____

_____

_____

Changes in setting_____

_____

_____

Descriptions of conflicts and resolutions _____

_____

_____

Themes that run throughout the story, like love, friendship, loyalty, good vs. evil, perseverance, revenge, envy, and courage_____

_____

_____

Writing a Standard Book Report *(cont.)*

The Four Parts of a Book Report *(cont.)*

Part 3—The Conclusion

The conclusion recounts the end of the story. It tells how the conflict is resolved and what happens to the characters.

Part 4—The Evaluation

The evaluation is your chance to give your opinion about the book. It may contain compliments, criticism, or a mixture of the two. Use the following questions as a guide to write your evaluation.

1. Do you think this book would interest other readers of your age? Explain why or why not.

   _____

   _____

   _____

2. Do you think this book will appeal to readers with special interests?

   _____

   _____

   _____

3. Have you read any other books by this author? If so, which ones?

   _____

   _____

   _____

4. Would you like to read other books by this author or other books on the same subject? Explain why or why not.

   _____

   _____

   _____

The Writing Process

Check and date each step as you complete it.

	Completed	Date
1: Pre-Writing Use the notes you made as you read to complete the pre-writing activities on pages 11–13.		
2: First Draft Transfer the information to your own paper, writing complete sentences and using present tense verbs. Read your report out loud to yourself.		
3: Second Draft Revise your paper by making changes and corrections. Read your paper aloud again. Does it make sense? Is it clear to you? Ask another person to read your revision. Rewrite any sentence that the reader thinks is confusing so that your writing is clearly understood.		
4: Final Editing Check your report for spelling, punctuation, grammar, etc. Use the Book Report Check List on page 20 as a guide. Make corrections and rewrite your report for the final time.		
5: Complete your cover page. It should include the name of the book, the author's name, your name, class period, date, etc.		
6: Assemble the report. Read through your report for the last time; make sure the pages are in order		

Food for Thought: It is a good practice to make an extra copy of your report for yourself

Book Report Checklist

❏ **Capitalization**—Have you capitalized the first word of each sentence as well as the proper names of people and places?

❏ **Punctuation**—Have you used end marks and other punctuation correctly?

❏ **Paragraphing**—Have you indented each new paragraph?

❏ **Spelling**—Have you verified spelling for each word?

❏ **Grammar**—Have you observed the rules of grammar?
Check for complete sentences, subject-verb agreement, pronoun-antecedent agreement, misplaced modifiers, and consistent verb tense.

❏ **Language**—Have you avoided informal language and slang?

❏ **Book Title**—Have you underlined (or italicized) the title of the book throughout your report?

❏ **Copy**—Is your finished product professional-looking?

❏ **Deadline**—Have you met your deadline?

❏ **Paper**—Is your paper fresh, unwrinkled, and unsmudged?

❏ **Writing**—Is your ink dark and handwriting easy to read?

❏ **Word-processing**—Have you used a standard, legible font with good pitch size (12–14)?

❏ **Margins**—Are the margins even on the top, bottom, and both sides of the page?

❏ **Personal data**—Have you included your personal data (name, class period, date, etc.) on the cover page to ensure proper credit?

❏ **A Final Check**—Now that you have a finished product, give thought to how you will assemble your report. Is a folder required? Is your paper securely stapled? Are your pages numbered in the correct sequence?

Food for Thought: Take pride in your work and turn in a report that is your best effort. A paper that has been proofread will often receive a higher letter grade than a non-proofread paper.

Quick and Easy Book Report

This short form may be used when a short book report is required, (for example, to accompany an oral presentation, or as assigned by the teacher). Use the information gathered on the pro-active reading note pages and follow the process on page 19 to complete this form.

Title: _____ Author: _____

Publisher: _____ Copyright date: _____

Introduction: _____

_____

_____

_____

Body: _____

_____

_____

_____

_____

Conclusion: _____

_____

_____

_____

Evaluation:_____

_____

_____

_____

_____

Surviving an Oral Presentation

To Think About: What is your first reaction when you learn you will have to give an oral report? Check the description that best fits you.

_____ I enjoy giving oral reports in front of my classmates because I am a good speaker.

_____ I can give oral reports in front of my classmates, but I don't enjoy it.

_____ I would rather not give an oral report because I get too nervous.

To Do: Follow the steps below to improve your oral report skills.

Preparing the Report

Transfer information from your written report to the outline form on page 23. Use the outline to prepare the index cards to use as speaking prompts. Do not write every word from your report on the cards. Use key words or phrases.

Controlling Your Nerves

Public speaking can make some people very nervous. Try the following techniques to help you deal with nervousness:

- Breathe deeply before you begin to speak.
- Position your feet comfortably and don't "lock" your knees.
- Relax your hands so that you are not clenching your cards.
- Remember that you are not alone—your classmates will have to give oral reports, too.
- Practice your report beforehand for added confidence.
- Number your cards in case you drop them.

Perfecting Your Posture

Practice your posture in front of a mirror and check for the following:

- Stand tall (but not rigid) and think of yourself as a professional person speaking in front of a group of business people. Avoid slouching or leaning.
- Look at your audience, not at your cards or the floor. If making eye contact causes you to giggle or stammer, look at a point just above the audience's heads.
- Clothing can affect your posture, so wear clothing that makes you feel confident and comfortable on your oral report day.

Developing Your Voice

Practice giving your report to a friend or family member, or tape-record your presentation. Use the following questions to critique your delivery.

- Are your diction and enunciation clear? Can the listener understand your words?
- Are you speaking too slowly or too quickly?
- Will people in the row farthest from you be able to hear you?
- Are you repeating phrases or sounds that will be a distraction to your audience like "you know," "well," "um," and "uh"?

Food for Thought: Employment areas in which good public speaking skills are essential include education, business, broadcasting, performing arts, law, and politics.

Cue Card Outline

Use one or two cards for each of the following topics. Copy the outline titles and add one or two words from your written report or pre-writing pages as prompts for each subtopic.

---

1. Write your opening sentence word for word.
2. Introduction/Exposition
   A. Setting
      1. (Time) _____
      2. (Place) _____
   B. Main Characters
      1. _____
      2. _____
   C. Theme(s)
      1. _____
      2. _____

---

3. Body (Plot)
   A. Beginning of the Book (Rising Action)
      1. _____
      2. _____
   B. Plot Development/Continuing Rising Action (Midway through the Book)
      1. _____
      2. _____
   C. Conflicts
      1. _____
      2. _____
   D. Turning Point/Climax of the Story
      1. _____
      2. _____

---

4. Conclusion/Resolution
      1. _____
      2. _____
5. Evaluation
      1. _____
      2. _____

In the Hot Seat

Your Name: _____

For this oral report you must become one of the main characters in the book you have read. You will need to take on the "persona" (character traits, style, and mannerisms) of your character. You may even want to dress in the way you think your character might dress.

To Do:

1. Write three to five questions for each of the categories below that will help your classmates learn about the plot, setting, theme, other characters, conflicts, and resolutions.

2. Put each question on an index card and distribute them to your classmates.

Take your place on the "hot seat" and let the questioning begin.

Be prepared to answer each question with as many details as possible.

Who?	What?
_____	_____
_____	_____
_____	_____

Where?	When?
_____	_____
_____	_____
_____	_____

Why or How?

_____

_____

Readers Theater

Before a book can become a film or play, a script must be prepared. You can practice turning a scene into a script to be presented as Readers Theater. In this format, the readers interpret the characters, using only their voices and other physical clues to bring the characters to life.

Work in a small group with others who have read the same book.

1. Select a passage from your book that involves action or conflict and contains enough dialog, or direct quotations, to be easily adapted. The scene should be complete and self-contained.

2. Write a brief introduction that a narrator or one of the speakers will read. It should set the stage for what is to follow, and answer the following questions: who, what, where, when, and why.

3. Prepare the script. Copy the lines each person will read. If there are descriptive passages, assign them to a narrator, or modify a character's speech to include essential information. Write the name of the character who speaks each line in the left margin, using capital letters.

4. Read through the script, taking parts, to make sure that it is complete and that it makes sense.

5. Type the script, if possible. Duplicate the script, making enough copies for all group members and one for the teacher.

6. Assign roles to members of the group. As a group, practice reading your script until you are familiar enough with the lines to look at the audience occasionally. It is not necessary to memorize all of your lines. Remember to use your voice and facial expressions to convey the character's emotions, attitude and mannerisms. Ask your teacher to listen to a read-through and make suggestions. You may want to tape-record a practice session so you can hear how it sounds.

7. When you are ready, perform your Readers Theater for your classmates. Arrange to have chairs or stools at the front of the classroom. You may want to stand at a podium to read.

P. O. P. Organizer

P.O.P. assignments are three-part book reports that require a *project*, an *oral report,* and a *presentation*. Use this form as a check list to help you plan and organize your P.O.P. assignment. You may be required to check-in with your teacher to report on your progress.

Book Title: _____

Author: _____

Project Name: _____

Due Date: _____ Completed: _____

Requirements

Project Plan: Decide what you will create. List all the materials you will need and make a rough sketch (if applicable).

Book Report: Organize the information from your pre-writing pages in a rough draft form. This will be used to create an oral report. Your teacher may prefer a brief written report instead of an oral report. Use the form on page 21.

Project Description: Provide a detailed description of the project. Explain what materials you used, the process you used, and anything you learned from the experience.

Presentation Note Cards: Transfer information about your book to index cards, using the outline form on page 23. Make a second set of cards from your written project description. Include a statement telling how your project reflects the book.

Book Covers

To Think About: Do you sometimes select a book because the cover looks interesting? Publishers use the covers of paperback books and the paper jackets on hard cover books to attract readers. Imagine that you are the cover artist for the book you have read. It is your job to create a cover that will capture the interest of other readers your age. The publisher has asked you to make a poster-size cover that will be used to sell the book.

Materials: poster board, markers, paints, crayons

To Do:

Project—Create a cover on the poster board for the book you have read. Use eye-catching colors and graphics that tell something about the book that will entice potential readers. Include the title, author, publisher's name and date of publication.

Oral Report—Use your reading notes to prepare an oral report on index cards (see page 23) or a brief written report.

Presentation—Display your poster and deliver an oral book report. See pages 21–24 for help in preparing and presenting an oral report.

Record the titles of books on which your classmates are reporting. Use the Oral Report Log below or a separate sheet of paper. Briefly take notes and put a star next to titles you may be interested in reading in the future.

Oral Report Log

Student Name	Book Title	Notes
1. _____	_____	_____
2. _____	_____	_____
3. _____	_____	_____
4. _____	_____	_____
5. _____	_____	_____
6. _____	_____	_____
7. _____	_____	_____
8. _____	_____	_____
9. _____	_____	_____
10. _____	_____	_____

Book-in-a-Box

Due Date _____

To Think About: As you read, make a chapter by chapter list of items that are mentioned in the story. Make a note of each item's significance. When you have finished reading, collect as many of these items as possible to use for your presentation. If you cannot find an item, draw it or cut a picture of it from a magazine.

Materials: shoebox or other medium-sized box, magazines, scissors, glue, and markers

To Do:

Project—Cover the box and its lid with pictures, words, and phrases that help tell the story of your book. Include the title of the book and the name of the author. Place the small items you have collected inside the box.

Oral Report—Use the information from your oral or written report to complete the Synopsis Notes below. Transfer your notes to a large index card.

Presentation—Follow the format for an oral report, page 23. Display each item at the appropriate point in your report and explain its significance to the story. After you have given your report, display your box of items and Synopsis card in the classroom.

Synopsis Notes

Title: _____

Author: _____ Date published: _____

Theme: _____

_____

Setting: _____

_____

Main Characters: _____

_____

Plot Summary: _____

_____

Conclusion: _____

_____

Evaluation: _____

_____

Other Times, Other Places

Reading books that are set in another country and/or in a different time period allows you to travel without leaving home. You can learn about customs, traditions, and daily life in other countries and expand your knowledge of the world and its people. Reading multicultural literature removes geographic borders and opens the door to new understanding. Multicultural reading also includes stories about people who live in America but retain the culture of their birthplace.

To Do:

Project—Create a poster, a travel brochure or other visual aid that will depict the culture that is represented in your book.

Oral Report—Prepare cue cards for your oral presentation.

Presentation—Explain the significance of your visual aid in understanding a different culture. Additional ideas to enhance your presentation:

- Play indigenous music of the culture represented in your book.
- Learn an indigenous dance or children's game and teach it to your class.
- Wear authentic clothing of the culture.
- Prepare an edible dish so that your classmates can sample food of the culture.
- Demonstrate a craft project and tell about its origin.

Around the World

- African
- African-Caribbean
- Asian (Chinese, Japanese, Hmong, Vietnamese, Korean, Filipino)

- European
- Middle Eastern (Egyptian, Israeli, Indian, etc.)
- Latin-American

- Native-American
- African-American
- Asian-American
- Jewish
- Hispanic-American

Authors of Multicultural Books

- Brent Ashabranner
- Joyce Annette Barnes
- Patricia Beatty
- Judith Ortiz Cofer
- Linda Crew
- Christopher Paul Curtis
- Nancy Farmer
- Doris Gates
- Virginia Hamilton

- Angela Johnson
- Helen Kim
- Lois Lowry
- Floyd Martinez
- Nicholasa Mohr
- Walter Dean Myers
- Uri Orlev
- Katherine Paterson
- Ami Petry

- Johanna Reiss
- Isaac Bashevis Singer
- Gary Soto
- Suzanne Fisher Staples
- Frances Temple
- Rita Williams-Garcia
- Laurence Yep

Fiction Fun with Fine Arts

Due Date _____

To Do:

Project—Select one of the options listed below, or think of a project of your own.

Music	Write a song about a character in the story or about a specific episode. Perform it live or prerecord your composition.
	Prepare an instrumental piece that depicts some aspect of the story.
Dance	Present a dance that portrays a character in the story.
	Present a dance that tells of a conflict and its resolution.
Poetry	Make a book of poems about the characters and incidents in the story. Assemble it in a creative way.
Art	Make a mini-mural that depicts some aspect of the book.
	Make sketches of the characters from your book and assemble them as a photograph album.
	Do a watercolor painting of the story's setting.
Woodwork, clay, sculpture	Make a model of a significant item in the story.
Sewing	Make a quilt and use appliqué or fabric paints to add highlights of the story.
	Create dolls for the main characters.

Oral Report—Prepare cue cards for an oral book report.

Presentation—Explain the significance of your project to the book. Perform or display your completed project.

On the Silver Screen

Many books have been made into movies. If the book that you read has not been made into a film, choose option A. If it has been made into a movie, choose option B for your report.

Option A

Imagine that you are the author of the book you have just read. Suddenly the book becomes a best seller. Write a letter to convince a movie producer that your book should be made into a movie.

- Begin by introducing yourself as the author and giving a brief summary of the story.

- Explain why the story, characters, conflicts, etc. would make a good film. Tell what age groups you think would want to see this film. Remember that movies are also made for television. You must decide if the movie will be shown in theaters, on prime time television, or as an after-school presentation.

- Make some suggestions for filming locations that would enhance the story.

- Suggest the names of the actors that you feel would best portray the major characters in your book, and tell why you would select them.

Option B

After you have read the book, watch the film version. Pretend that you are an actor, and that you would like to star in a re-make of the film. Write a letter to a producer comparing and contrasting the book to the existing movie.

Explain why you think this story should be re-told. Tell what things you would change to make the story better and to appeal to audiences. Make suggestions for changes in the point of view, casting, script, etc. You may also want to change technical aspects of the film, like adding technicolor or stereo sound.

Last, but not least, explain why you are the perfect person to star in this movie. Describe yourself and draw a comparison to the character.

Front Page News

To Do: Create a front page to a newspaper that is devoted entirely to the book you read. The front page should look as much like a real newspaper as possible with writing in columns, headlines, pictures, a newspaper title, etc. Everything you include, however, must be based on the setting, events, and characters in the book you read. Articles must be typed.

Ozark Mountain Times
Volume 1, Issue 1

10-Year Old Bags Gold Credits Hounds

Mountain Lion Claims Lives of Dan and Ann

- Design a masthead for your newspaper. The masthead includes the name of the paper, the place where it is published, and the date.

- Summarize the plot of the book you have read for the lead, or most important, article on the front page. Review your notes to find answers to these five questions the reader may have about the story.

  Who is the story about? _____

  What happened? _____

  Where did it happen? _____

  When did it happen? _____

  Why did it happen? _____

  How did it happen? _____

- Use the answers to the questions above to write a first draft of your article. Write a paragraph for each question, telling the story vividly, with as much detail as possible.

- Rewrite your article. Add an introductory paragraph that summarizes the article. Arrange the paragraphs in order of the importance of the information to the reader.

- When you are satisfied with your news article, write a headline: a brief phrase designed to catch the interest of the reader. Copy your headline and lead article to the front page. Add pictures, if desired.

- Fill the page with other articles based on the setting and characters in the book, like a weather forecast or a feature story on one of the more interesting characters.

If several members of the class have read the same book, you may decide to create an entire newspaper based on that book. Add more pages that include a variety of newspaper features, like an editorial, a letter from a character to the editor, a collection of ads that would be pertinent to the story, horoscopes for each character, "Dear Abby" letters, comic strips, news articles, personal ads, an obituary section, etc.

Book Reviews

To Think About: A book review is a reader's critique of a book. Reviews can be found in newspapers, magazines, and on the Internet. They help other people decide which books they will read. To give a thorough book review, one must look at the book objectively. Follow these steps to write a book review.

1. Look at the cover of the book that you have read. Try to remember why you chose this book. What did you think it would be about? On a separate sheet of paper, write about your feelings after reading the story. Was the book what you expected it to be? Do you still feel the same about the book? What has changed?

2. Give a brief description of the book. Tell about the main characters and the setting, as well as what the story is about (don't give away the good stuff or the ending). Include information about the type of book (e.g., historical fiction, fantasy, nonfiction, etc.) and who the author is.

> The Westing Game by Ellen Raskin
>
> Great, page turning mystery!
>
>
>
> Sam Westing has just died. 16 people are gathered at the old Westing House for the reading of his will. They are surprised when the will turns out to be a game. One of these 16 people is Sam Westing's murderer and one is the heir to his fortune. Follow the clues to solve the mystery. The characters are not who they seem to be. I found this book addicting after the few first chapters. It is a spine-tingling, white-knuckle, page-turning book. Don't be misled by these characters. Read this book!!!!!!!!!!

3. Next, give at least two reasons why you either liked or disliked the book. Be sure to give an example to clarify your feelings and be sure to justify your feelings.

4. In closing, you might remind the reader again whether you liked or disliked the book and give a recommendation to the reader to either read it or not. It is also helpful at this point to state the age group for which you feel this book is appropriate.

5. How would you rate this book? Give your book a star rating from one to five, five being best.

6. Write a headline or a one-line summary about the book.

7. If you have access to the Internet, go to **http://www.barnesandnoble.com** or **http://www.amazon.com**. These are Web sites for bookstores. Once you have found one of these sites, type the title of your book at the prompt that says "keyword."

8. Click on the book title. Scroll down the page to the section labeled "Customer Comments."

9. Click on the prompt that asks if you would like to add a review. Follow the directions on the screen and type your review in the boxes.

10. **Teacher Note:** Preview web sites before students publish their reviews. As an alternative, use written reviews to create a class literary journal and review.

What's Your URL?

You have been asked to create a Web site devoted to the book that you have read. Follow the steps below to prepare your site.

1. Decide on a name for your Web site.

2. Use the name to complete a URL, or address, where people can find the site.
   http://www. _____.com

3. The first page that people logging into your site will see is the home page. Create a brief introduction to the book and add an illustration. You will also need to provide a menu or listing of the topics covered on each following page. If you wish, you may add a graphic for each topic.

4. Write and illustrate a page for each of the following: the story (summary), the characters, the setting, a review (evaluation) and the author. Decide on a layout for each page.

5. Provide a page of links to other web sites that are related to your book. They may be other book sites, author pages, information about the setting of the book, or pages that a character might visit.

6. The last page of your web site is the "Guestbook." Invite those who visit your site to sign their names and leave a brief message.

7. Use colored paper, pencils and markers to draw a picture of each web page. The text for each page must be typed. Paste it on the page.

8. Staple the pages together. Exchange web booklets with other students in your class. After reading the material, sign the guestbook page.

Literary Pen Pals

Dr. Doolittle
"Animal Communicator"

Mrs. Basil E. Frankweiler

Samuel W. Westing

Captain Nemo
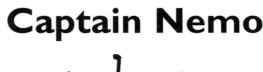

To Do: Write a letter from a character, using letterhead stationary that you have designed for the character.

1. Design a letterhead for stationery that is appropriate for the main character of your book. It should include the character's name and a design or symbol that represents his or her talent, occupation, or achievement.

2. Review the book and identify incidents that reveal the character's personality and the situation.

3. Pretend that you are the character. Write a letter to a distant friend or relative (your real self) telling about the problem you are facing.

4. Remember to write from the character's viewpoint. Use language appropriate for the character and the situation. Show the character's personality by the manner in which he or she responds to people, places and conflict. Use a date and setting appropriate to the story or incident.

5. Describe the problem that you, the character, are facing. Explain who or what is complicating the situation. Tell what or who is helpful in solving the problem.

6. Copy the letter to the letterhead.

7. Design a letterhead for yourself and answer the character's letter, offering suggestions and showing your support for your friend or relative. Remember that in this role you do not know the outcome.

8. Write a second letter from the character in which he or she responds to your letter and focuses on the change in the situation and him or herself.

9. Respond to the second letter.

Lights, Camera, Action

To Do: The book you have read has just been made into a movie and you have been hired to create an interesting, attention-getting preview that will make movie-goers all across the country want to see this new release.

- Prepare a script for your preview. Begin by selecting scenes from different parts of the book. Remember that previews should not reveal whole scenes or the conclusion of the story. Plan to give the viewer quick glimpses of what the movie is about.

- One useful planning tool is a storyboard. Decide what will be covered in each scene. Make a sketch of the action. Assemble the sketches in order on a large piece of poster board.

- To get the attention of your audience and create interest, have a narrator ask a question, describe a situation, etc.

- Enlist some friends to act out your script. Practice, and then record your preview on videotape.

- Add appropriate background music that fits the overall mood or atmosphere of the movie. Create an interesting visual design of the title and videotape it at the end of the preview. Add credits, including the author and publisher as well as the actors and actresses (Use the names of professionals or those of your friends.) who star in this feature film.

- When your project is complete, arrange with your teacher to have a screening for your class. Turn in the script with this project.

1	2	3	4

_____ _____ _____ _____

_____ _____ _____ _____

_____ _____ _____ _____

_____ _____ _____ _____

Something to Celebrate

Pretend that you are planning a party for the characters in the book you read. Complete each of the following tasks to plan your party.

1. Decide what kind of party is appropriate, based on an event in your book. It may be a birthday party (or an un-birthday party), housewarming, anniversary, holiday celebration, graduation day, etc. You may also choose a theme for the party, if you wish.

   Type of party: _____ Theme: _____

2. Select a day, date, time, and location for the party. Consider what you know about the setting and the schedules of the characters. Fill in the invitation below. Add appropriate decorations.

3. Plan a menu for the party. Explain why each item is appropriate for the character and/or the theme of the party.

4. How will you decorate for the party? Describe your decorations.

   _____

   _____

5. Tell what games or entertainment you will provide and why your choices are appropriate.

   _____

   _____

6. Choose five of the characters in the book. Tell what each one would wear to the party.

7. Predict how three of the characters will act at the party.

Use the blank form below to invite someone to your party.

Classic Character Mobile

To Think About: After reading a classic novel, think about how the characters in the book might react to living in your world. What problems would they face? Could they adjust to a new life-style? Would their lives be easier or more difficult?

Materials: magazines, hangers, string or yarn, glue, scissors, glitter, markers, heavy construction paper or poster board

To Do: Look through current magazines to find faces that could be modern versions of the characters in the book. Cut out a picture for each character and glue it to heavy paper, leaving a border or frame around the picture. Decorate the borders with symbols that represent the characters. Punch one hole in the top of each frame and one in the bottom of each frame.

Cut smaller pieces of heavy paper and make nametags for the characters. Punch a hole in the top of each nametag.

Thread the hole in each nametag with a piece of string or yarn and tie it to the picture frame.

Thread another piece of yarn or string through the hole at the top of each frame and attach the frames to the hanger.

King Arthur

Discuss your character mobile in a small discussion group or with the whole class. Use the following questions to guide your discussion.

- Would the characters change or remain the same in a contemporary setting? Explain why or why not.

- What contemporary solutions to conflicts would be available to the characters?

- What new problems would the characters face in a modern setting?

- Considering personality traits and characteristics, which characters would be good employees in today's work force?

- Which characters would you like to have as friends? Explain your choices.

- Which character would benefit the most from living in the contemporary setting?

Food for Thought: How would you like to live in your character's world? What adjustments would you have to make? What advantages or disadvantages would someone your age experience?

Biography Banner

To Think About: Who is the most interesting person you have ever met? Have you ever met a famous person? A biography is the life story of a famous or interesting person written by another person. There may be several biographies by various authors about a person who has had a great impact on history.

There are several reasons for reading about other people's lives.

- We can learn about history and expand our knowledge of the world and its people.
- We can learn about great accomplishments and heroic deeds.
- We can gain an appreciation of the great talents and personalities of people who lived in other times.
- We can explore careers and lifestyles that other people have already experienced.

Materials: dowel for hanging the banner; sturdy fabric (e.g., burlap, felt, or canvas); and paints, markers, yarn, etc., for decorating

To Do: Select and read a biography about someone who interests you. See the suggestions below. As you read, fill in the "Life at a Glance Time Line" boxes (page 40). Make a banner that depicts an important aspect of the person's life.

The finished banner should be at least 24" x 24" (61cm x 61 cm). Include the title of the biography and important dates, as well as pictures and patterns in your design.

Finding a Biography

Use the card catalog in the library. If there is someone you admire or about whom you would like to learn, search for him or her by name. You may also select a subject area that interests you and search for related biographies. Here are some ideas to get you started.

Government and Politics—Justice William Rehnquist, Dr. Martin Luther King, Jr., Abraham Lincoln, Nelson Mandela, Sitting Bull, Barbara Jordan, Cesar Chavez

The Arts—Agnes De Mille, Louis Armstrong, Norman Rockwell, Mark Twain, Aaron Copland, William Shakespeare, Zora Neal Hurston, Paul Robeson, E.B. White

Medicine—Clara Barton, Florence Nightingale, Jonas Salk, Dr. Christian Barnard, Louis Pasteur, Joseph Lister

Humanitarian—Pope John Paul II, Mother Teresa, Albert Schweitzer, Reverend Billy Graham, Danny Kaye

Science and Inventions—Albert Einstein, Joseph and Marie Curie, Thomas Alva Edison, Alexander Graham Bell, George Washington Carver

Sports—Roberto Clemente, Babe Ruth, Babe Didrikson Zaharias, Michael Jordan, Wayne Gretzsky, Muhammad Ali

Exploration and Adventure—Chuck Yeager, Charles Lindbergh, Sally Ride, Neil Armstrong, Jacques Cousteau, William Lewis, Amelia Earhart

Life at a Glance Time Line

To Do: Use this form to record significant events and dates from the life of the subject of your book. As you read, record events and their dates in each stage of the subject's life. After you have completed the book, identify significant dates and contributions or projects and summarize these on the back of this page.

Time line for _____

Birth	Childhood	Youth

Adult	Later Years	End of Life

40

Book Words

Word Bank

antagonist	chapters	editor	library	printer	synopsis
author	characters	epilogue	literature	proofread	theme
binding	conflict	fiction	nonfiction	protagonist	typeface
biography	copyright	foreshadowing	novel	publisher	
book report	denouement	graphics	plot	sequel	
card catalogue	Dewey Decimal System	librarian	preface	setting	

Across
3. numbers from 0–999 used to classify books
5. clues
8. in the land of imagination
10. how pages of a book are kept together
13. reading/writing assignment
15. an explanation that introduces a book
19. just the facts
25. the great body of reading material
27. the pattern of events in a narrative story
31. where and when a story takes place
32. a book's artwork

Down
1. person who prepares a book for publication
2. can help you find books
4. makes multiple copies for readers
6. 400-year-old literary form
7. an adversary
9. the main character in a book
11. a story's final outcome
12. a continuation of a story
14. a problem within or without
15. puts the book into print
16. writer

17. a life story
18. assists in finding answers to difficult research questions
20. people portrayed in a book
21. material protected by the law
22. a book's postscript
23. a summary
24. divisions in a book
28. the writer's main idea
29. the kind of print used for a book
30. quiet zone

Integrating Films and Videos with Reading

To Think About: There never seems to be enough time for your students to read all the books on your list of favorites. One way to squeeze in a few more books each year is to use "books-on-film" or videos. With some careful planning, you can create high interest learning days to increase your students' awareness of great authors and books.

When to show a book-on-film: A book-on-film can be used to celebrate after students have completed a major report, project, or unit of study. Videos can also be used effectively on the day or two preceding a school vacation and on field trip days when a large number of students are away.

The benefits of using older films: Older films are generally more conservative and suitable for middle school classroom viewing. Some are in black and white and others are in "Technicolor," but special effects are limited. As an added benefit, your students can learn about the history of filmmaking and meet some of yesterday's great film stars.

Planning a Book-On-Film Day

1. Make copies of the appropriate viewing guide for each student. Use the form on page 43 if the video is of a book that the students have read. If you are using the video to introduce the students to a book that they have not read, use the form on page 44.

2. Put the following information on the board: names of characters, title of the film/book, author, date of book's publication, date of film's release, setting (time and place). State a clear objective for viewing this film.

3. Have students fill in this information before the film begins. Leave enough light on for students to work on their film guide sheets.

4. Collect film guide sheets for credit to encourage good listening skills. If time permits, discuss the film and the students' opinions and observations.

Suggested Viewing List

Title	Release Date	Title	Release Date
20,000 Leagues Under the Sea	1954	Lassie Come Home	1943
A Christmas Carol	1951	Little Women	1933, 1996
A Connecticut Yankee in King Arthur's Court	1949	My Friend Flicka	1943
Black Beauty	1971	National Velvet	1945
Black Stallion	1979	Old Yeller	1957
Born Free	1966	The Adventures of Huckleberry Finn	1960
Clash of the Titans	1981	The Adventures of Tom Sawyer	1938
Diary of Anne Frank	1959	The Count of Monte Cristo	1974
Doctor Doolittle	1967	The Invisible Man	1933
Excalibur	1981	The Lion, the Witch and the Wardrobe	1979
Fantastic Voyage	1966	The Little Prince	1974
Farewell to Manzanar	1976	The Miracle Worker	1962
Golden Voyage of Sinbad	1974	The Three Musketeers	1948
Gulliver's Travels	1976, 1998	The Wizard of Oz	1939
Ivanhoe	1952, 1982	Time Machine	1969
Jason and the Argonauts	1963	Treasure Island	1950
Johnny Tremain	1957	Ulysses	1955
Knights of the Round Table	1953	Yearling	1946

Film Viewing Guide 1

Objectives for viewing this film: _____

Title of film: _____ Year released: _____ Produced by: _____

Title of book film is based upon: _____ Author: _____

Characters: _____

_____

Setting: _____

_____

Sequence of events (plot/conflicts):

1. _____
2. _____
3. _____
4. _____
5. _____
6. _____
7. _____
8. _____
9. _____
10. _____

To Think About: Reading a book first and then seeing a film/video which has been made from the book, can put you in the critic's seat. As a reader, you have formed a mental image of the characters, setting, and plot elements. The filmmaker may have had a different vision. You must also be aware that when a book is rewritten as a film, some scenes may be omitted. Ask yourself the following questions as you critique the film:

1. Make a list of the similarities (comparing) and differences (contrasting) between the movie and the book. Write one or more short paragraphs telling how the plot, characters, setting, conflicts, etc., are alike and how they are different.

2. In what ways was the book better? In what ways was the film better?

3. Did the moviemaker stay close to the original story?

4. Do you think the book's author would be pleased with this filmed rendition of his/her book?

Film Viewing Guide 2

Title of film: _____ Year released: _____ Produced by: _____

Title of book film is based upon: _____ Author: _____

Characters: _____

_____

Setting: _____

_____

Sequence of events (plot/conflicts):

1. _____
2. _____
3. _____
4. _____
5. _____
6. _____
7. _____
8. _____
9. _____
10. _____

To Think About: Most books must be modified or adapted in order to make a movie from them. Filmmakers rely on the camera to provide information on the setting, and narration often becomes dialogue. In the case of a long book, scenes may be condensed or eliminated.

1. What did you think about the story? Were you satisfied with the ending?

2. Describe your favorite character from the movie. Is he or she someone you would like to know better? Tell why.

3. Summarize the plot. Was it believable?

4. Give specific examples of things you liked or disliked in the film.

5. What parts of the film would you like to know more about? Do you plan to read the book? Explain why or why not.

Reading Connections Across the Curriculum

With some additional planning, you can heighten student interest, extend learning, and get more "mileage" from the novel your class is reading by using this planning page before reading begins. Refer to your planning page throughout the course of reading and add more ideas as they come to you. Remember to use your areas of interest, special talents, and abilities as you use this page.

Title: _____

Author: _____ Genre: _____

Connections to

Related Literature
Author
Title
Topic

Science
Environment
Other

Social Studies
History
Geography

Visual and Performing Arts
Film/Stage
Music
Painting
Dance
Sculpture

Themes, Human Interest

Math

People
Customs
Culture
Food
Clothing
Life-style

Student Interests

Current Events
Global
National
Local

Idea Bank and Notes

How to use the Student Report Packet: Copy pages 8–15 and assemble a packet for each student. To make finding a specific page easier, color-code the pages to designate tracking pages, writing pages, etc. Pages should be hole-punched and kept in a binder to encourage neatness and organization skills. Have extra copies of the pro-active reading pages and the report pre-writing pages available for additional reports.

Reading/Reporting Portfolio: As students complete each book report assignment, collect the written reports and file them in a Reading/Reporting Portfolio. At the end of the year, return the portfolios with a certificate of achievement.

Oral Book Reports: Enlist the help of a student and have him or her give an oral report that demonstrates distracting behaviors, poor posture, etc. If you wish, ask a second student to give the same report using the techniques presented on page 22. Let the class critique the reports.

Readers Theater: Arrange to have the students perform their project for another class.

How to use the P. O. P. Pages: These are three-part reports that require a project, an oral or written report and a class presentation. Make copies of page 26 and the specific project page for each student. Discuss the requirements for the assignment, including the type of report, and set deadlines. Provide copies of page 23 for oral reports or page 21, the Quick and Easy Report Form.

Book Cover Project: Display your Book Cover Posters in the school library, cafeteria, or other visible location. Arrange the jackets alphabetically by author, or in chronological order using either the date of original publication or the current edition date.

Front Page News: Page 32 may be modified to create a cooperative project in which students contribute articles about different books to create a whole newspaper. Include a wire service style dateline at the beginning of each news article. A second alternative would be to present the articles orally, following the format of a national news broadcast or television news magazine.

Biography: Banner Biographies can come alive if someone acts as a news reporter and interviews the person. Video tape several interviews in a television journal style.

On-line Review: If two students have read the same book, pair them to present a "Thumbs Up, Thumbs Down" discussion. Follow the popular movie-rating format. Each student will summarize the book and give his or her opinion. Conclude the presentation by rating the book "Two Thumbs Up," "One Thumb Up, One Thumb Down," or "Two Thumbs Down."

Photo Record: Take photographs of students and projects throughout the year. Display the photos to create high interest and positive anticipation of future reports.

Celebrate Reading: Have your students bring snacks and drinks to share on deadline days or on the last day of oral presentations. Set aside a corner of the classroom as a library. You will need shelves for books and displays of student projects. If space permits, add floor pillows or comfortable chairs for readers.

Sample Letters

To Do: Use the sample letter below to ask for help in building your classroom library.

> Dear Friends,
>
> I am in the process of building a class library in my classroom and would appreciate your help in acquiring books for my students. Please consider donating any used books for young adults that you no longer need.
>
> As you go to garage/yard sales, would you keep my students in mind when you spot a book that you think would be good for our library?
>
> My goal is to promote a life-long enjoyment of reading by providing easy access to good books in my classroom.
>
> Thank you for joining me in this goal.
>
> Sincerely,

To Do: Make a list of friends, colleagues, and community leaders who would be good "guest readers" in your class. Possible choices include coaches, the principal, business leaders, community leaders and elected officials, television and radio personalities, local authors and journalists. Use the sample letter below, or write your own letter, to invite your guest readers.

> Dear _____,
>
> As a _____ grade teacher at _____
> School, it is my goal to instill in my students an interest and appreciation in reading good books. You can help me achieve this goal for my students by being a Guest Reader in our classroom.
>
> Please consider coming to my school for a one-time reading session in which you would read aloud a short story or poem. We would be honored to have you as one of our reading role models. If you are interested and able to participate, please contact me at my school _____, home _____, or e-mail me at_____.
>
> I look forward to hearing from you.
>
> Sincerely,

After a visit from a guest reader, have your students write thank you letters. Make a "Wall of Fame" with photographs of guest readers, taken when the reader was in your class.

Reading Resources

Books

Amazon.Com
http://www.amazon.com
Barnes and Noble
http://barnesandnoble.com

Bks. Educational Paperbacks
http://www.bksbooks.com (800-854-8508)
BMI Educational Services,
http://www.bmiedserv.com/ (800-222-8100)

Special Websites for Readers

America Reads Challenge
http://www.ed.gov/inits/americareads/
(800-USA-LEARN)

Pizza Hut Book It!
http://www.bookitprogram.com/index.html
(National Reading Incentive Program, includes a
bibliography to grade 7, 10 theme-related
categories 800-426-6548)

Resources for Special Needs

**National Library Services for the Blind
and Physically Handicapped (NLSBPH)**
http://lcweb.loc.gov/nls/nls.html
1-800-424-8567   1-202-707-5100

American Foundation for the Blind
http://www.afb.org/afb
National Center for Learning Disabilities
http://www.ncld.org/welcome.html

Additional On-line Resources

Book club on-line,
http://www.smplanet.com/bookclub/interactive/index.html
Book lists and links to other websites at The Mining Company
http://yabooks.about.com/mbody.htm
Information about authors and illustrators
http://www.author-illustr-source.com/
Internet School Library Media Center (ISLMC)
http://falcon.jmu.edu/~ramseyil/childlit.htm
Multicultural books
http://scholar.lib.vt.edu/ejournals/ALAN/fall95/Ericson.html
Book Reviews, author information, etc.
http://www.carolhurst.com/index.html

Crossword Puzzle—Page 41

Across

3. Dewey Decimal System
5. foreshadowing
8. fiction
10. binding
13. book report
15. preface
19. nonfiction
25. literature
26. proofread
27. plot
31. setting
32. graphics

Down

1. editor
2. card catalogue
4. printer
6. novel
7. antagonist
9. protagonist
11. denouement
12. sequel
14. conflict
15. publisher
16. author
17. biography
18. librarian
20. characters
21. copyright
22. epilogue
23. synopsis
24. chapters
28. theme
29. typeface
30. library